Writing with Grace

Second Edition

Michael McHugh

**Christian Liberty Academy
Handwriting Program**

Written by Michael J. McHugh
Copy editing by Christopher Kou
Cover design by Robert Fine
Layout and graphics by **imagineering studios, inc.**

A publication of

Christian Liberty Press
502 West Euclid Avenue
Arlington Heights, IL 60004
www.christianlibertypress.com

ISBN 978-1-930367-88-3
            1-930367-88-0

Text set in Berkeley
Handwriting set in Zaner-Bloser except for "Q" and "k," and ","
Printed in the United States of America

Contents

Cursive Development Group I: Difficult Lowercase Letters

Manuscript Maintenance

Cursive Development Group II: Uppercase A-N

Cursive Development Group III: Uppercase O-Z

Lowercase Cursive Alphabet

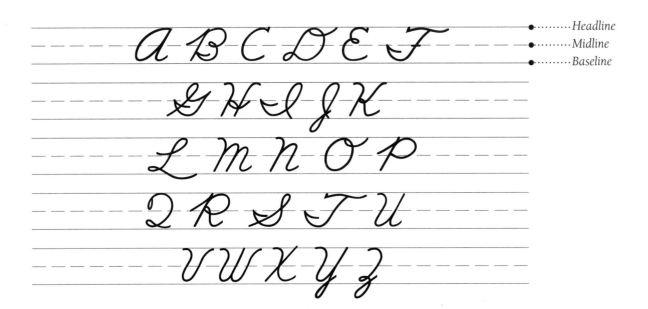

a b c d e f
g h i j k
l m n o p
q r s t u
v w x y z

• ········ Headline
• ········ Midline
• ········ Baseline

Uppercase Cursive Alphabet

A B C D E F
G H I J K
L M N O P
Q R S T U
V W X Y Z

• ········ Headline
• ········ Midline
• ········ Baseline

Numbers

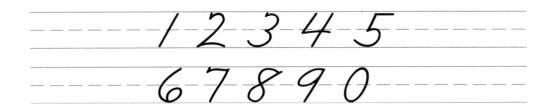

1 2 3 4 5
6 7 8 9 0

Preface

This is the fourth text in the Christian Liberty Academy handwriting series. This text will extend and reinforce the cursive handwriting skills previously presented in the series. It will also encourage the students to keep up their manuscript handwriting skills by showing the practical applications of these skills.

We remind you that one key to teaching success is reducing frustration in both parent and student. A wise teacher will not fail to take into account the maturity of the children so they can enjoy their handwriting activities without constant boredom or extreme fatigue.

Learning can and should be fun. The staff at Christian Liberty Academy has taken care to design each lesson to fit the attention span of the average primary student.

Patience, prayer, and persistence are indispensable for success at teaching primary handwriting. It is very important for instructors to realize that extra drill work (on the blackboard and practice paper) must be assigned for each and every concept in the textbook.

This text selects only the 40 letters that are most difficult for students: the capitals and lowercase a, b, e, h, i, k, m, n, o, p, r, s, t, and v. If other letters cause your students difficulty, the exercises are easily adapted to other letters.

Both gross and fine motor skills are involved in handwriting. Certain abilities are generally found at this level of development:

1. Ability to follow a series of spoken or written directions.
3. Ability to color within lines.
4. Ability to draw figures such as circles and squares.
5. Ability to distinguish between left and right.

This text contains activities to develop and maintain the above skills.

Good handwriting is an essential skill of expression and communication. Time spent on handwriting is well spent. May the God of all grace help you develop students who will desire to write legibly and attractively for the glory of God.

In Christian fellowship,
Michael J. McHugh

Introduction to Parents

In this text you will be asking your students to take more responsibility for their handwriting skills. This text will cover the principles of advanced cursive. Therefore, you will be asking your students to evaluate their own developing writing ability.

Before you begin, make sure your students have the proper readiness skills:

1. Can the students hold the pencil in a correct fashion?
2. Do the students recognize the difference in forms of letters and words?
3. Do the students appreciate handwriting as a means of communication?
4. Are the students reasonably able to copy a letter?

To improve fine motor skills and eye-coordination, make sure your students have ample opportunity to cut and paste, use paint brushes, draw with chalk on a board, create with clay, play ball, build with blocks, hammer pegs, and finger-paint. All these playful activities develop and strengthen the skill necessary for handwriting.

Proper forming of letters requires complete relaxation of all the muscles not directly involved in the act of writing: the fingers and wrist should be relaxed, not tense. The forearm should pivot on the elbow to direct hand and pencil along the horizontal line of the paper.

To help students get ready to write, they should be taught to:

1. Sit up straight, leaning forward slightly
2. Rest both arms on the desk
3. Keep both feet on the floor
4. Relax

Handwriting will improve if practiced every day. Fifteen to twenty minutes a day is sufficient at this grade level. If the student is improving at a slower pace than is reasonable, chances are that the student needs more time doing readiness activities first. Don't be tempted to increase handwriting practice time–when readiness skills are developed enough, the student will improve in handwriting skills most efficiently without being pushed.

Left-Handedness

Make sure your students are using the hand that is most natural for them. If you are unsure, watch to see which hand your student uses to reach for things, which foot starts a flight of stairs, which hand he uses to throw a ball, and with which hand the student has the best fine motor skills (coloring, inserting a key, picking up a coin). The hand that predominates is the hand to be encouraged. Remember that left-handed students will have a more difficult task, because the movement from left to right across the page is awkward for the left hand.

Pretest

Chapter Check-up

Are you ready to write? Do your best work as you copy these phrases in cursive.

please work quickly   **big fuzzy musk ox**   **white candy vase**

Queen Kate Washes Xylophones?   **Isaac Adored God**   **Ezekiel Derided Baal**

Answer the following questions.   Circle

1. Do all my letters slant in the same direction?	Yes	No
2. Am I shaping every letter correctly?	Yes	No
3. Are all the letters in one word connected?	Yes	No
4. Am I spacing letters evenly?	Yes	No
5. Am I leaving space between words?	Yes	No
6. Am I leaving extra space between sentences?	Yes	No
7. Am I remembering punctuation?	Yes	No
8. Am I remembering to capitalize?	Yes	No

Letters I write well:

Letters I need to practice:

rake

bored

Practice the small letter "**r**." The strokes are shown to get you started.

Practice the small letter "**b**." The strokes are shown to get you started.

Write the word "**rub**" ten times.

Write the word "**burr**" ten times.

Provide extra practice as needed on separate lined paper.

4

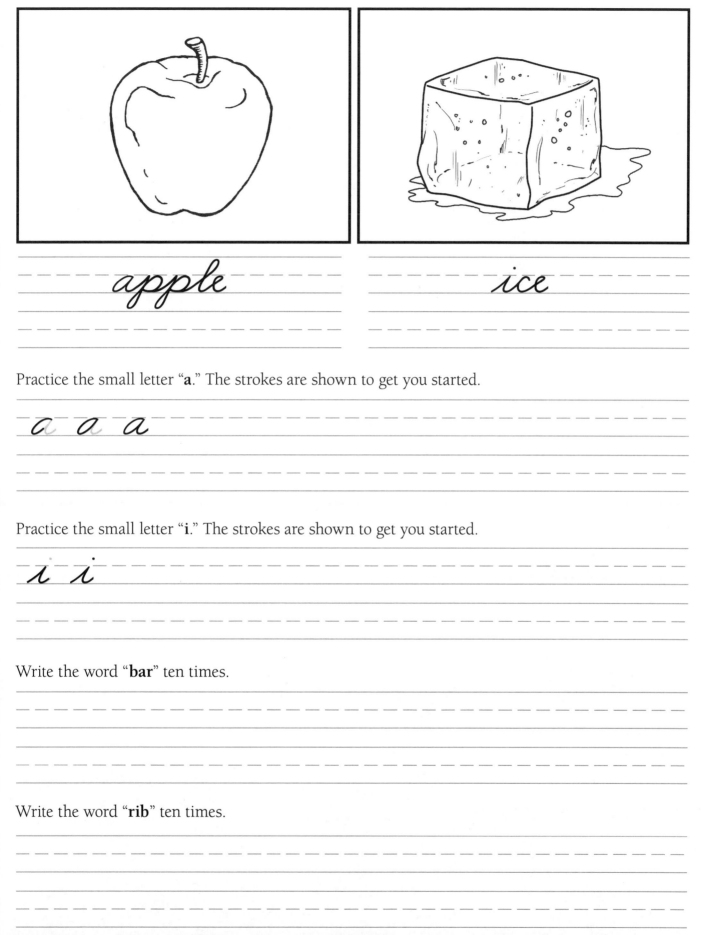

apple

ice

Practice the small letter "**a**." The strokes are shown to get you started.

a a a

Practice the small letter "**i**." The strokes are shown to get you started.

i i

Write the word "**bar**" ten times.

Write the word "**rib**" ten times.

Provide extra practice as needed on separate lined paper.

kitten

high

Practice the small letter "**k**." The strokes are shown to get you started.

k k k

Practice the small letter "**h**." The strokes are shown to get you started.

h h h

Write the word "**ark**" ten times.

Write the word "**hair**" ten times.

Provide extra practice as needed on separate lined paper.

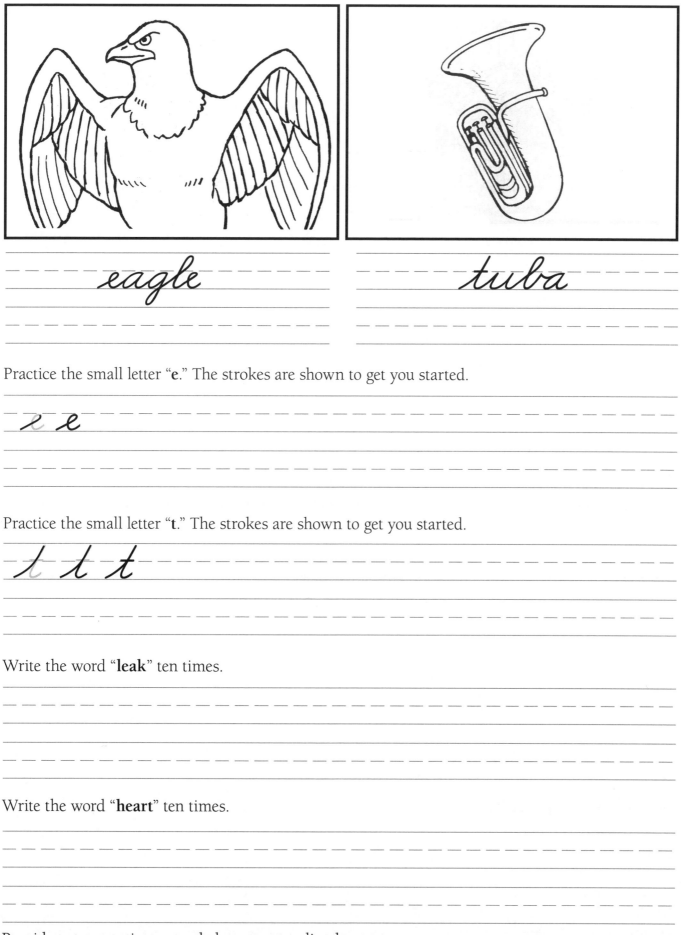

eagle

tuba

Practice the small letter "**e**." The strokes are shown to get you started.

e e

Practice the small letter "**t**." The strokes are shown to get you started.

t t t

Write the word "**leak**" ten times.

Write the word "**heart**" ten times.

Provide extra practice as needed on separate lined paper.

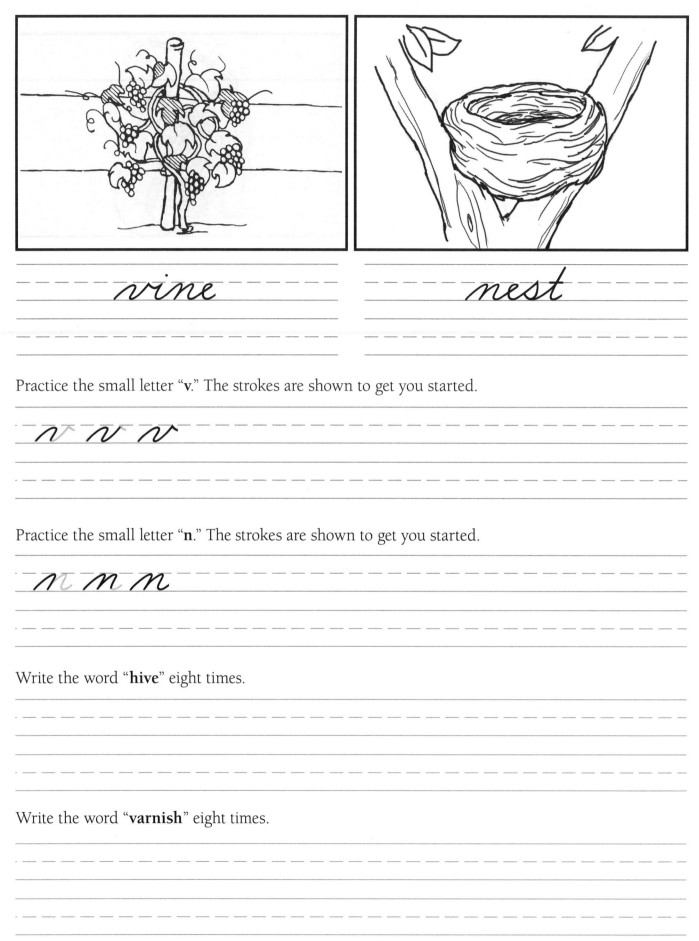

vine

nest

Practice the small letter "**v**." The strokes are shown to get you started.

Practice the small letter "**n**." The strokes are shown to get you started.

Write the word "**hive**" eight times.

Write the word "**varnish**" eight times.

Provide extra practice as needed on separate lined paper.

minuteman   *oatmeal*

Practice the small letter "**m**." The strokes are shown to get you started.

m m m m

Practice the small letter "**o**." The strokes are shown to get you started.

o o

Write the word "**making**" eight times.

Write the word "**ivory**" eight times.

Provide extra practice as needed on separate lined paper.

paste   *straw*

Practice the small letter "**p**." The strokes are shown to get you started.

p p p p p

Practice the small letter "**s**." The strokes are shown to get you started.

s s s

Write the word "**popsicle**" eight times.

Write the word "**strawberries**" five times.

Provide extra practice as needed on separate lined paper.

Homonyms

Some words sound alike but are written differently. To be understood, we must know how to write the word we mean.

to: in the direction of
too: also; more than enough
two: the number 2
hear: to sense through the ear
here: in this place

their: belonging to them
there: in that place
they're: they are
your: belonging to you
you're: you are

Choose the word in (parentheses) whose meaning fits. Copy the whole sentence.

I went (to, too, two) church.

_____

Four is (to, too, two) many.

_____

The book is over (their, there, they're) on the table.

_____
_____
_____

(Their, There, They're) coming tomorrow.

_____

Come over (hear, here).

_____

I (hear, here) the bells ringing.

_____

I borrowed (your, you're) pencil.

_____

Bonnie thinks that (your, you're) right.

_____
_____

There are many more homonyms. How many can you think of?

_____
_____
_____
_____

Opposites (Antonyms)

Writing is both easier and more fun when we are used to thinking of the relationships between words in form and meaning.

Make the sentence say the opposite by replacing the word in **heavy type** with its opposite (its antonym). Rewrite the whole sentence.

My coffee is too **cold**.

_____

- -

The blanket is **over** the bed.

_____

- -

Some people sleep during the **night**.

_____

- -

_____

- -

We live in a **little** house.

- -

_____

I wish I had **fewer** books.

- -

_____

Goliath was a **tall** man.

- -

_____

The angel food cake tastes **bad**.

_____

- -

_____

- -

Our team members are **good** losers.

_____

- -

_____

- -

Compound Words and Prefixes

Some words join together to make a new word with a new meaning.

Combine the words in (parentheses) to make a word that fills the blank.
Rewrite the whole sentence

(wear under) I put on warm _____ in the winter.

- -

(ache in the head) All that thinking gave me a _____ .

- -

(book for notes) Write it in your _____.

- -

(house for a club) Our _____ is in Jody's garage.

- -

Some parts of words, such as prefixes, never stand alone. They join with words or
other word parts to make new words.

Replace the words in **heavy type** in each sentence with a single word. Make the new word from
one of the words in the sentence and one of these word parts:

re	again
un	not yet
over	too much
under	not enough

Rewrite the whole sentence.

I had to **work** the problem **again**.

- -

May **cooked** the spaghetti **too much**.

- -

Play that tape **again**.

- -

Jim's bed was **not made yet**.

- -

Treatment of homonyms, antonyms, compound words, and prefixes is light here because the topics are more pertinent to
grammar than to handwriting.

13

Solve the Clues

Write the word that matches the meaning. Here is the word list:

true   cross   save   seek   walk   belief   pay   try

Travel on foot

Faith

Go from one side to the other

Look for

Not false

Give money that is owed

Rescue

Now try these:

arm   cow   house   bowl   ship   rocket   play

Round dish that can hold liquid

Four-footed animal that gives milk

Upper limb of the body

Seagoing vehicle

Have fun

Building in which people live

Space vehicle

Codes

Can you decode the messages? Here is the decoder:

A = 1	J = 10	R = 18
B = 2	K = 11	S = 19
C = 3	L = 12	T = 20
D = 4	M = 13	U = 21
E = 5	N = 14	V = 22
F = 6	O = 15	W = 23
G = 7	P = 16	X = 24
H = 8	Q = 17	Y = 25
I = 9		Z = 26

13-1-11-5 8-1-25 23-8-9-12-5 20-8-5 19-21-14 19-8-9-14-5-19.

4-15-14'20 16-21-20 1-12-12 25-15-21-18 5-7-7-19 9-14 15-14-5 2-1-19-11-5-20.

1 16-5-14-14-25 19-1-22-5-4 9-19 1 16-5-14-14-25 5-1-18-14-5-4.

Codes

Can you decode the messages? Here is the decoder:

A = 1	J = 10	R = 18
B = 2	K = 11	S = 19
C = 3	L = 12	T = 20
D = 4	M = 13	U = 21
E = 5	N = 14	V = 22
F = 6	O = 15	W = 23
G = 7	P = 16	X = 24
H = 8	Q = 17	Y = 25
I = 9		Z = 26

1-13 9 13-25 2-18-15-20-8-5-18'19 11-5-5-16-5-18?

1 19-15-6-20 1-14-19-23-5-18 20-21-18-14-19 1-23-1-25 23-18-1-20-8.

9 1-13 20-8-5 22-9-14-5, 25-15-21 1-18-5 20-8-5 2-18-1-14-3-8-5-19.

Create Words

See how many words you can make using the letters in the word below. Use each letter only once for each word. One word is **pop**. Try to make at least ten words.

Hippopotamus

Try this word: **Elephant**

Create Words

See how many words you can make using the letters in the word below. Use each letter only once for each word. One word is **nose**. Try to make at least ten words.

Rhinoceros

Try this word: **Pachyderm**

Abraham Lincoln

Abraham Lincoln's school was his very own home. Most of our country's great leaders were schooled in small one-room school houses. In your best penmanship, describe some of the blessings of learning at home.

> Let the word of Christ dwell in you richly in all wisdom; teaching and admonishing one another in psalms and hymns and spiritual songs, singing with grace in your hearts to the Lord.
>
> ~Colossians 3:16

Teaching Notes

Help your students with difficult connecting strokes. Practice on extra paper should be encouraged. If a student needs practice on lowercase letters other than those presented here, build exercises like the preceding to provide practice.

How Am I Learning?

Are you ready to write? Do your best work as you copy this sentence.

We voted last spring to buy a sack of hamburgers.

Answer the following questions.   Circle

1. Do all my letters slant in the same direction?   Yes   No
2. Am I shaping every letter correctly?   Yes   No
3. Are all the letters in one word connected?   Yes   No
4. Am I spacing letters evenly?   Yes   No
5. Am I leaving space between words?   Yes   No
6. Am I leaving extra space between sentences?   Yes   No
7. Am I remembering punctuation?   Yes   No
8. Am I remembering to capitalize?   Yes   No

Letters I write well:

Letters I need to practice:

Crossword Puzzle Exercise

Crossword puzzles are one place we use manuscript even in adulthood. They are also good exercise for the brain and for vocabulary.

Answer the clues to fill in the crossword. The number on the clue tells you where to start the answer in the puzzle. Some answers go across, and some go down.

Down
1. A girl's name
2. Opposite of under
3. Gave way for a short time
4. Finishes

Across
1. Part in a play
5. A place to bake
6. After a letter is written, you _____ it.
7. Painting is one of these

Now try this one.

Down
1. Amount of money to pay
2. A bar to hold a wheel
3. Something necessary
4. Also

Across
1. The place of Jesus' first miracle
5. Animals that pulled covered wagons
6. A thing in which to ride across snow
7. A boy's name

Filling Out Forms

Even as adults we must use manuscript to fill out forms. Two forms that children often fill out are applications for library cards and bicycle registration forms.

BICYCLE REGISTRATION CARD

PLEASE PRINT	DATE OF REGISTRATION

(LAST)   (FIRST)   (INITIAL)

NAME OF OWNER

HOME ADDRESS	TELEPHONE NUMBER
MAKE	WHEEL SIZE

		CHECK ONE:
MODEL	MODEL NUMBER	☐ BOY'S
		☐ GIRL'S
COLOR	TRIM COLOR	☐ DELIVERY

OTHER IDENTIFICATION

NAME AND ADDRESS OF PARENT OR GUARDIAN (LAST, FIRST, M.I.)

NAME AND ADDRESS OF PERSON FROM WHOM PURCHASED	DATE PURCHASED

LIBRARY CARD APPLICATION

PLEASE PRINT

last name	first name	middle initial

address	city	state	ZIP

age	grade	school

X _____
signature

phone

Write a Headline

You are a newspaper editor! In your best printing, write a headline for each paragraph. A good headline is short, but it covers the most important facts in the story or the paragraph.

_____
_ _
_____

Our dog, Sarah, had puppies yesterday. There were four puppies. Two looked like her, and one looked like it's father. One was a mixture of Sarah and the other dog. Their names are Ruff, Peewee, Scarf, and Missy.

_____
_ _
_____

Last week the Templetons went to the museum. They spent most of the time looking at the Indian exhibit, because Jaime and his sister, Lois, are interested in Indian homes and costumes. One thing they saw was a Pawnee earth lodge. The Pawnees lived in Nebraska in houses made of earth. They moved to Oklahoma in 1876.

_____
_ _
_____

Three things needed for fishing are bait, a hook, and some line. A pole makes fishing easier, but it is not needed. Worms are a good bait for many fish, but some fish like insects, minnows, or crayfish. It is very important to be quiet when fishing. Fish can hear in the water, and they will not bite if they are frightened.

_____
_ _
_____

Benjamin Franklin was one of the men who helped organize the colonies into the United States. He accomplished many things. He wrote and printed a magazine called "Poor Richard's Almanac," he invented a more efficient stove for heating, and proved that lightning and electricity were different forms of the same thing. He was also an accomplished swimmer. He was not too shy to try anything that caught his interest.

_____
_ _
_____

There were no horses in America when the first settlers arrived from Europe. All the horses in America are settlers from Europe, too. Most of the wild horses here came from horses that escaped from the Spanish explorers. Before the Europeans brought horses to America, the Plains Indians hunted buffalo on foot.

Making an Outline

The reason for making an outline is to show how ideas fit together. Making an outline is a good way to begin writing. All our decisions about what to say are made in the outline before we get off on the wrong foot.

Read these paragraphs and then fill in the outline in your best printing.

My Family

I have two parents; a mother and a father. My father works as a carpenter, and sometimes he goes to meetings at our church at night. My mother works at home, cleaning, paying bills, cooking meals and teaching me.

I have an older brother and an older sister. My brother's name is John. He likes to play basketball and is good at spelling. My sister's name is Anne. She likes to play tennis and is good at arithmetic.

I. My Parents

    A. Father

details about my father

        1. work: _____

        2. another thing he does: _____

    B. My Mother

work my mother does at home

        1. _____

        2. _____

        3. _____

        4. _____

II. Brothers and Sisters

    A. Brother

        1. Name: _____

        2. Something he likes: _____

        3. Something he's good at: _____

    B. Sister

        1. Name: _____

        2. Something she likes: _____

        3. Something she's good at: _____

Write a Title for the Pictures

In your best cursive penmanship, give each picture a title. A good title is short, but tells enough to let someone know what is most interesting about the picture.

The first, second, fourth, and fifth pictures represent biblical places and people. Picture 1 is Bethlehem (Mt. 2:1-12, Lk. 2:1-20). Picture 2 is David (2 Samuel). Picture 4 is Jacob and Esau (Gen. 25:29-34). Picture 5 is Peter walking on the water (Mt. 14:22-33). If your students have not heard these Bible stories, they may have trouble with this exercise.

Thomas Alva Edison

Did you know that Thomas Edison was taught at home by his mother? Tom learned at an early age to make good use of his time. In your best penmanship, tell about two of Thomas Edison's many inventions. Explain how these inventions affect how we live today.

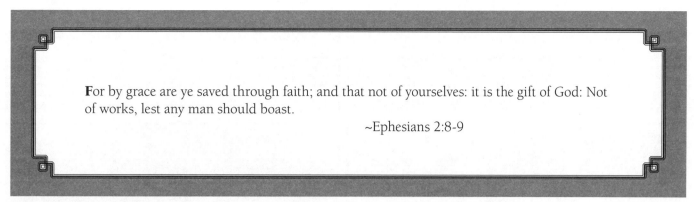

For by grace are ye saved through faith; and that not of yourselves: it is the gift of God: Not of works, lest any man should boast.

~Ephesians 2:8-9

Teaching Notes

If your students' manuscript is not firm, build exercises like the preceding to provide more practice.

How Am I Learning?

Are you ready to write? Use your best printing as you copy this sentence.

With a quick jerk, the big fuzzy musk ox pulled the cart into view.

Answer the following questions.   Circle

1. Am I keeping all letters on the baseline?   Yes   No
2. Am I shaping every letter correctly?   Yes   No
3. Am I making each letter the correct height?   Yes   No
4. Am I spacing letters evenly?   Yes   No
5. Am I leaving space between words?   Yes   No
6. Am I capitalizing and using periods or question marks?   Yes   No
7. Am I leaving extra space between sentences?   Yes   No

Letters I print well:

Letters I need to practice:

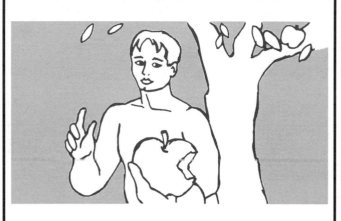

Adam

Bethlehem

Practice the capital letter "**A**." The strokes are shown to get you started.

a a a a

Practice the capital letter "**B**." The strokes are shown to get you started.

B B B B B

Write the word "**Able**" ten times.

Write the word "**Boston**" eight times.

Provide extra practice as needed on separate lined paper.

Calvary

Daniel

Practice the capital letter "**C**." The strokes are shown to get you started.

C C

Practice the capital letter "**D**." The strokes are shown to get you started.

D D D D

Write the word "**Cain**" ten times.

Write the word "**Denver**" eight times.

Provide extra practice as needed on separate lined paper.

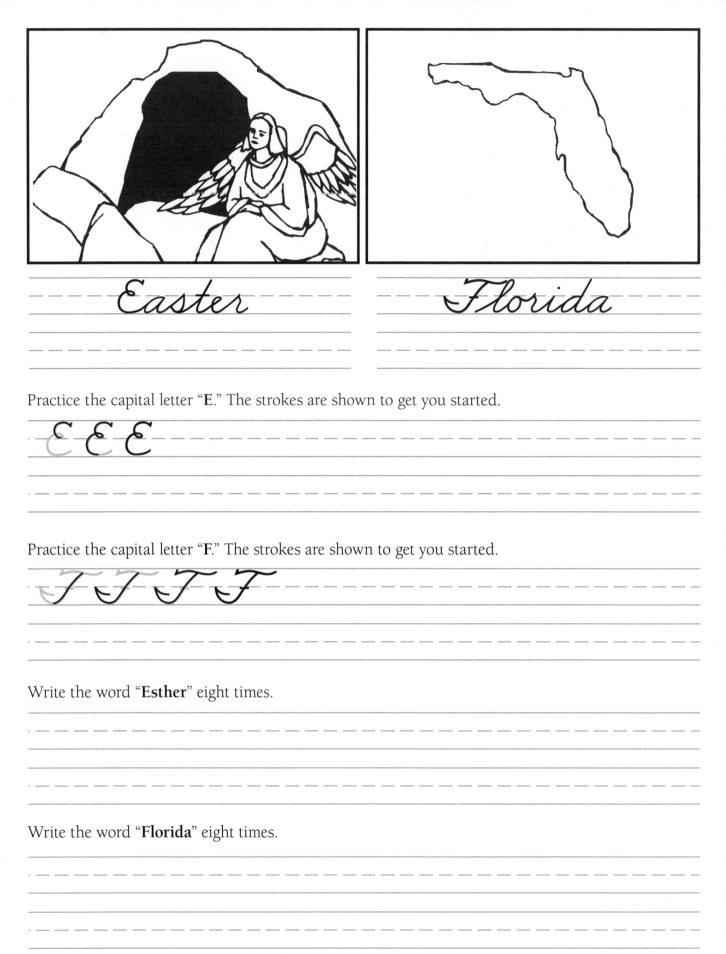

Easter

Florida

Practice the capital letter "**E**." The strokes are shown to get you started.

$\mathcal{E}$ $\mathcal{E}$ $\mathcal{E}$

Practice the capital letter "**F**." The strokes are shown to get you started.

$\mathcal{F}$ $\mathcal{F}$ $\mathcal{F}$ $\mathcal{F}$

Write the word "**Esther**" eight times.

Write the word "**Florida**" eight times.

Provide extra practice as needed on separate lined paper.

Goliath   *Hospitality*

Practice the capital letter "**G**." The strokes are shown to get you started.

G G G G

Practice the capital letter "**H**." The strokes are shown to get you started.

H H H H

Write the word "**Georgia**" ten times.

Write the word "**Horeb**" ten times.

Provide extra practice as needed on separate lined paper.

Isaac

Jacob

Practice the capital letter "**I**." The strokes are shown to get you started.

Practice the capital letter "**J**." The strokes are shown to get you started.

Write the word "**Isaac**" eight times.

Write the word "**Jackson**" eight times.

Provide extra practice as needed on separate lined paper.

King David

Lazarus

Practice the capital letter "**K**." The strokes are shown to get you started.

K K K K

Practice the capital letter "**L**." The strokes are shown to get you started.

L L L L

Write the word "**Kankakee**" eight times.

Write the word "**Lot**" eight times.

Provide extra practice as needed on separate lined paper.

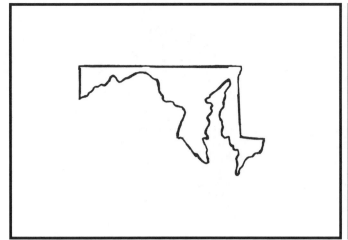

Maryland

Noah

Practice the capital letter "**M**." The strokes are shown to get you started

M M M M

Practice the capital letter "**N**." The strokes are shown to get you started.

N N N

Write the word "**Maine**" ten times.

Write the word "**Noah**" ten times.

Provide extra practice as needed on separate lined paper.

Quotations

Quotation marks are used to signal that words belong to someone other than the writer.
The most common use is to mark quoted speech.
Look at this sentence: **Jesus said, "I am the Way."**
     The mark " shows where Jesus' words begin. The mark " shows where His words end.
     Put quotation marks where they belong. Copy the whole sentence.

Do you want to come with me? Uncle Ed asked.

_____

_____

My mom said, Excuse me. Can you let me by?

_____

_____

Cory, Dad exclaimed, this is very fine work!

_____

_____

All my baby sister can say is ba-ba.

_____

_____

Behold, Jesus said, I am coming soon.

_____

_____

Unscramble the Poem

The students should use both rhyme and meaning to do this exercise. The rhyme scheme is **aabb**.

The lines of these poems are scrambled. Can you sort out the lines so they make sense? Copy the poems when you have unscrambled them.

He went as fast as he could go.
He had a dollar for a treat,
Bobby went to see the show.
So he could eat while in his seat.

_____

_____

_____

_____

She bought three bags of chips or more.
She walks and sings a birthday tune.
Her birthday party's very soon,
Jean went to the grocery store.

_____

_____

_____

_____

Alphabetizing

This is the first of two alphabetizing exercises in this text. The students should get more practice in their language arts or English instruction. The exercise is primarily for handwriting practice.

In the dictionary and in the telephone directory, words are in alphabetical order. Words that begin with "**a**" come first, then words that begin with "**b**," and so on.

These words are in alphabetical order:

        ax   boy   car   dog   eat   fry   go   home   ice   jet

Write these words in alphabetical order: bone   door   ask   cat

Try these: pan   nation   open   mail   quite

Try this group. It's a little harder, because some letters are skipped in the alphabetical order.
bone   eagle   cart   go

Try these: pan   eagle   open   cart   bone

Now try this group. The order is much more spaced out.
telephone   man   woman   house

Try these: zoo   apple   open   fill   spin

Try just one more: north   zebra   kind   ant   monkey   giraffe

Homonyms

Some words sound alike but are written differently. To be understood, we must know how to write the word we mean.

led: showed the way   **desert**: wasteland
lead: a soft metal   **dessert**: sweets after a meal
every day: each day   **capital**: city where government meets
everyday: common, ordinary   **capitol**: building where legislators meet

Choose the word in (parentheses) whose meaning fits. Copy the whole sentence.

Alice (led, lead) the way.

_____

_____

Some houses have pipes made of (led, lead).

_____

_____

The coleus is an (every day, everyday) plant.

_____

_____

I go to the grocery store (every day, everyday).

_____

_____

Jesus was tempted in the (desert, dessert).

_____

_____

For (desert, dessert) we had strawberry shortcake.

_____

_____

We sat in the gallery of the (capital, capitol) building.

_____

_____

Washington, D.C., is our nation's (capital, capitol).

_____

_____

Opposites (Antonyms)

Writing is both easier and more fun when we are used to thinking of the relationships between words in form and meaning.

Make the sentence say the opposite by replacing the word in **heavy type** with its opposite (its antonym). Rewrite the whole sentence.

Second Street is **smooth**.

_____

Elma's sister is **stingy** with her toys.

_____

_____

Jason **opened** the desk drawer.

_____

_____

My father walked **into** the room.

_____

_____

We are **likely** to be out of lemonade.

_____

_____

Working **carefully** results in **neat** papers.

_____

_____

My grandmother lives **close** to us.

_____

_____

_____

Compound Words and Prefixes

Some words join together to make a new word with a new meaning.

Combine the words in (parentheses) to make a word that fills the blank.
Rewrite the whole sentence

(light for the street) I must be inside when the _____ comes on.

— —

_____

(hole for a button) Threads are coming loose on my _____ .

— —

_____

(ache in the stomach) Janet ate too much chocolate and got a _____.

— —

_____

(coat to go over) Mother put on her _____, since it was cold.

— —

_____

Some parts of words, such as prefixes, never stand alone. They join with words or other word parts to make new words.

Replace the words in **heavy type** in each sentence with a single word. Make the new word from one of the words in the sentence and one of these word parts:

re	again
un	not yet or the reversing of an action
over	too much
under	not enough

Rewrite the whole sentence.

They decided to **run** the old show **again**.

_____

— —

Our swing set is **not used enough**.

_____

— —

The bike was **priced too high**.

_____

— —

The location for the Cub Scout dinner is **not decided yet**.

_____

— —

_____

— —

Quotations

This exercise was introduced on page 35. The subtleties of indirect discourse, the ironic use of quotation marks, and the like are beyond the scope of this text. Students should study those topics in English and language arts.

Quotation marks are used to signal that words belong to someone other than the writer.
The most common use is to mark quoted speech.
Look at this sentence: **"Nicodemus," Jesus said, "I am the Way."**
      The mark " shows where Jesus' words begin. The mark " shows where His words end.
      Put quotation marks where they belong. Copy the whole sentence.

Mark, Aunt Betsy said, I could use your help.

_____

_____

Amy, John asked, can you come over and play?

_____

_____

But the greatest of these, Paul wrote, is love.

_____

_____

If any man thirst, said Jesus, let him come to Me.

_____

_____

Nicodemus said to Jesus, How can a man be born when he is old?

_____

_____

Alphabetizing

This exercise was introduced on page 37. Students use the first two letters to alphabetize on this page. If your students have not had much practice alphabetizing, this page may prove confusing. Provide generous help if so, or defer the exercise until the students have acquired more experience.

How do we alphabetize words what begin with the same letter? We look at the second letter. These words are in alphabetical order:

able   acre   add   after   age   ahead   air   ajar

Write these words in alphabetical order: break   bean   bicycle   blue

_____

_____

Try these: man   mine   mutt   moon   meat

_____

_____

And these: not   neat   nut   nail   nice

_____

_____

Now try these: old   over   oak   on   open

_____

_____

Sometimes the first and second letters are both used to put words in alphabetical order. Note the example below.

able   acre   ball   call   crew   cut

Now try this group: act   but   and   band

_____

Try these: dune   cat   but   dot   bat   cut

_____

Next this: dune   act   dot   but   label   and   band

_____

_____

_____

Are you ready for a hard one? Try this: boil   meal   bill   made   bat   acre   bend   older   eat

_____

_____

_____

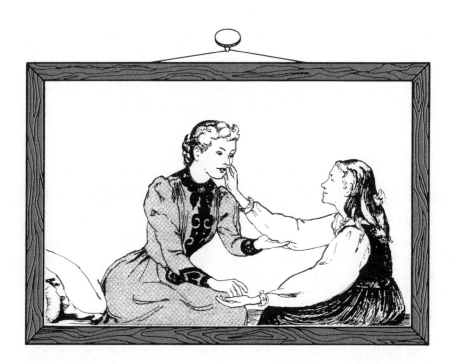

Helen Keller

Helen Keller was both blind and deaf from the time she was one year old. Her mother taught her at home. She learned to read and speak, and even went to college. She learned to use the talents and abilities God had given her. In your best penmanship, explain what the Bible means when it says, "To whom much is given, much will be required." [Luke 12:48]

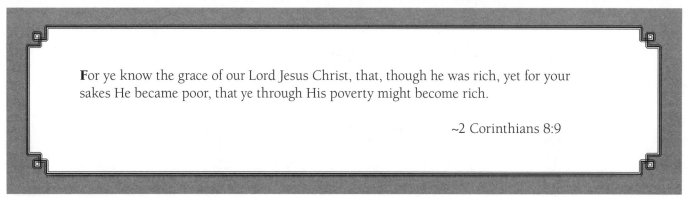

For ye know the grace of our Lord Jesus Christ, that, though he was rich, yet for your sakes He became poor, that ye through His poverty might become rich.

~2 Corinthians 8:9

Teaching Notes

Remember always to provide extra practice on ruled paper. Are your students applying what they learn about handwriting in tasks where the focus is not on handwriting?

How Am I Learning?

Are you ready to write? Do your best work as you copy each phrase.

Frances Called Katherine   Isaac Adored God   Ezekiel Derided Baal

Answer the following questions.   Circle

1. Do all my letters slant in the same direction?   Yes   No
2. Am I shaping every letter correctly?   Yes   No
3. Are all the letters in one word connected?   Yes   No
4. Am I spacing letters evenly?   Yes   No
5. Am I leaving space between words?   Yes   No
6. Am I leaving extra space between sentences?   Yes   No
7. Am I remembering punctuation?   Yes   No
8. Am I remembering to capitalize?   Yes   No

Letters I write well:

Letters I need to practice:

Obedience

Paul of Tarsus

Practice the capital letter "**O**." The strokes are shown to get you started.

$\mathcal{O}$ $\mathcal{O}$

Practice the capital letter "**P**." The strokes are shown to get you started.

$\mathcal{P}$ $\mathcal{P}$ $\mathcal{P}$ $\mathcal{P}$

Write the word "**Orlando**" eight times.

Write the word "**Philip**" eight times.

Provide extra practice as needed on separate lined paper.

Quarter

Rebekah

Practice the capital letter "**Q**." The strokes are shown to get you started.

Q Q Q

Practice the capital letter "**R**." The strokes are shown to get you started.

R R R R R

Write the word "**Queens**" eight times.

Write the word "**Rachel**" eight times.

Provide extra practice as needed on separate lined paper.

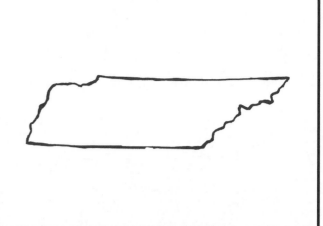

Simon Peter   *Tennessee*

Practice the capital letter "**S**." The strokes are shown to get you started.

Practice the capital letter "**T**." The strokes are shown to get you started.

Write the word "**Solomon**" eight times.

Write the word "**Trenton**" eight times.

Provide extra practice as needed on separate lined paper.

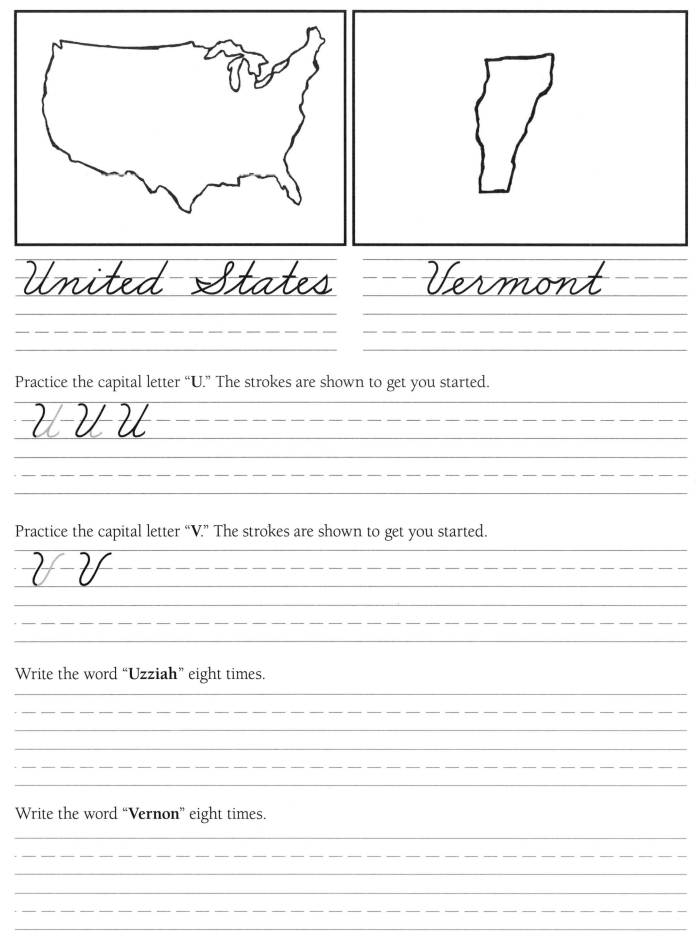

United States   *Vermont*

Practice the capital letter "**U**." The strokes are shown to get you started.

U U U

Practice the capital letter "**V**." The strokes are shown to get you started.

V V

Write the word "**Uzziah**" eight times.

Write the word "**Vernon**" eight times.

Provide extra practice as needed on separate lined paper.

 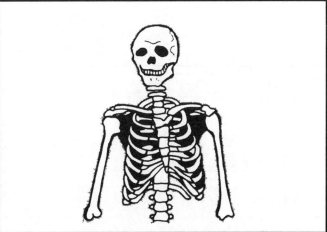

Washington *X-ray*

Practice the capital letter "**W**." The strokes are shown to get you started.

W W W W

Practice the capital letter "**X**." The strokes are shown to get you started.

X X

Write the word "**Warren**" eight times.

Write the word "**Xenia**" eight times.

Provide extra practice as needed on separate lined paper.

Yoke of Oxen

Zacharias

Practice the capital letter "**Y**." The strokes are shown to get you started.

Y Y Y Y

Practice the capital letter "**Z**." The strokes are shown to get you started.

Z Z Z

Write the word "**Yuma**" eight times.

Write the word "**Zebulun**" eight times.

Provide extra practice as needed on separate lined paper.

Writing a Business Letter

A business letter differs from a friendly letter only in the greater number of marks of courtesy in a business letter. The *return address* and the *inside address* are the most obvious additions. A *colon* is used after the salutation rather than a comma. The *tone* is more formal, the *language* more careful and reserved, and *titles* such as Mr., Mrs., and Dr. are observed. Usually, business letters are typed, again as a courtesy. Friendly letters are covered in book 3 of this series.

Notice the parts of this sample business letter. Also notice the business-like way the words are used.

Jerome Davis
return address 555 Oak Street
Arlington, VT 00004
date March 29, 2003

Richard Firling
Director, Customer Services
Edgebrook Toy Co.
55 E. Keystone Ave. inside address
Chicago, IL 60692

Mr. Firling: salutation

body

I am enclosing a Sonic Zoom Blaster I bought from a local store on January 29. The Zoom Blaster does not work, and the store has gone out of business and cannot help me. I would like Edgebrook Toy Co. to repair or replace my Sonic Zoom Blaster.

Thank you for your attention.

complimentary close Sincerely,
signature Jerome Davis

Copy the letter for practice.

51

Writing a Business Letter

Write your own business letter to Leonard Grayson, President of General Cereals, 5555 Hialeah Road NW, Jacksonville, TX 75222, asking for information on the free theme park tickets his company offers. You need to know how many box tops to send and to what address they should be sent.

return address

date

inside address

salutation

body

complimentary close

signature

Number Words

There are two kinds of number words–*cardinal* (meaning main, or basic) and *ordinal* (those that show order). These exercises will briefly review the ordinal numbers and good form in writing them when they are expressed in figures (as in "4th").

When putting things in order, we use words like "first" and "last". Every number has a special form (called **ordinal numbers**) to show order in the same way. Look at these pairs:

one–first	five–fifth
two–second	six–sixth
three–third	seven–seventh
four–fourth	eight–eighth

Rewrite the sentences on this page using numbers that show order. The words in the sentence may have to be changed around a little.

Example: Three people came before Andy in the line. Andy was **fourth** in line.

I fell on step number six.

_____

_____

Marcie ate cookie number five from the plate.

_____

_____

Five people have asked that question before Jill.

_____

_____

No one arrived before Joan.

_____

_____

I got in line behind fifteen other people.

_____

_____

More On Number Words

Sometimes we write ordinal number forms with numerals instead of with words. Numerals have ordinal forms too. An ending is taken from the word form of the ordinal and added to the numeral without any space. Look at the pairs in this list:

first–1st   sixth–6th
second–2nd   seventh–7th
third–3rd   eighth–8th
fourth–4th   ninth–9th
fifth–5th   tenth–10th

This kind of number is most common in dates. Answer the questions on this page in full sentences using the numeral form of the ordinal numbers.

On what day do we celebrate the birth of Jesus?

_____

_____

_____

_____

What day is George Washington's Birthday?

_____

_____

_____

_____

When is your birthday?

_____

_____

_____

_____

What day is Independence Day?

_____

_____

_____

_____

What day is it today?

_____

_____

_____

_____

Write a Sentence for the Pictures

In your best cursive handwriting, write a short sentence telling what is happening in each picture.

Making an Outline

In an outline, the most important ideas are written on the far left. Important ideas can be broken down into smaller ideas. Sometimes the smaller ideas can be broken down too. Each step in the breakdown is written a little farther right, so an outline looks a little like an upside-down staircase.

Read these paragraphs and fill in the missing information in the outline using your best printing.

God's Love

God shows His love in many ways. He created all human beings, starting with Adam and Eve, the first man and woman. He also made my mother and father, and gave them the power and gift to have children. God made me.

God also saves me from sin. He sent Jesus, His only Son, who died for my sins and wants me to accept Him as my Savior. God gives me grace, which helps me in three ways: it helps me to avoid sin, to know God's will, and to accept Jesus as my Savior.

God keeps me safe. He inspired Scripture, which protects me from doing things that make Him sad. He answers my prayers. His love is with me throughout my entire life and will sustain me into life everlasting.

God's Love

I. God created human beings
    A. God created Adam and Eve, the first man and woman.
    B. God gave my mother and father the power and gift to have children.

    C. _____

II. God saves me from sin.

    A. _____

        1. Jesus is God's only Son

        2. Jesus died for my sins

    B. God gives me grace.

        1. Grace helps me to avoid sin.

        2. _____

        3. _____

III. _____
    A. He inspired Scripture, which protects me from mistakes.
    B. He answers my prayers.

    C. _____

Making an Outline

The purpose of this exercise is largely handwriting practice. Do not hesitate to give generous help to students having difficulty relating outline form to sentences.

You have had help making outlines from paragraphs earlier in this book. Can you make an outline without help? Try it.

How David Became King

It may seem strange that David became king of Israel. David was the youngest son of Jesse. When he was young, he spent his days tending sheep.

Saul was king of Israel before David, but he lost his kingship. Saul had disobeyed the Lord. Samuel, the Lord's prophet, told Saul that he would no longer be king.

With the Lord's guidance, Samuel found David on Jesse's land. Samuel anointed David king of Israel. The Bible says that the Spirit of the Lord was on David from that time forward.

Saul did not want to give up the kingship. He often tried to kill David, and David was forced to live in hiding. Since God was with David, David finally became king.

David did not always live blamelessly, but when he sinned, he confessed his sins openly. When he was truly sorry, God forgave him.

Write a Story

Choose one of the titles below. Write a story to go with the title. You may also make up your own title and write a story to go with it.

My Favorite Song   **My Favorite Sport**   **The Best Meal I Ever Had**

What I Want to Be When I Grow Up

Laura Ingalls Wilder

Living on the frontier most of her early life, Laura Ingalls Wilder, who wrote the Little House books, did not often have the opportunity to go to school. She did not attend school regularly until she was eight years old. Her mother, however, loved to read to the family. From her mother's love of reading, Laura learned to love stories and poems. In your best penmanship, tell about two things you have learned to like because your parents like them.

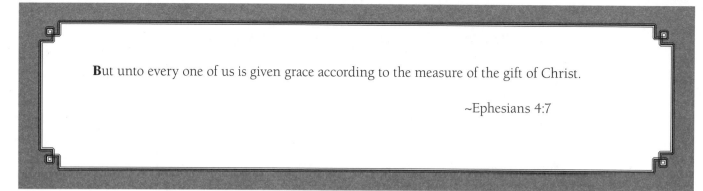

> **B**ut unto every one of us is given grace according to the measure of the gift of Christ.
>
> ~Ephesians 4:7

Teaching Notes

Remember always to provide extra practice on ruled paper. Are your students applying what they learn about handwriting in tasks where the focus is not on handwriting?

How Am I Learning?

Are you ready to write? Do your best work as you copy each phrase.

Very Rickety Toaster   **Simeon Prophesied about Young Jesus Zeke Washed the Oven**

Answer the following questions.   Circle

1. Do all my letters slant in the same direction?	Yes	No
2. Am I shaping every letter correctly?	Yes	No
3. Are all the letters in one word connected?	Yes	No
4. Am I spacing letters evenly?	Yes	No
5. Am I leaving space between words?	Yes	No
6. Am I leaving extra space between sentences?	Yes	No
7. Am I remembering punctuation?	Yes	No
8. Am I remembering to capitalize?	Yes	No

Letters I write well:

Letters I need to practice: